WORLD WAR II
TECHNOLOGY

BY LAURA K. MURRAY

CONTENT CONSULTANT
Kristie Macrakis
Professor in the School of History, Technology, and Society
Georgia Institute of Technology

Core Library

Cover image: The US B-29 Superfortress was the most
advanced heavy bomber of World War II.

An Imprint of Abdo Publishing
abdopublishing.com

abdopublishing.com

Published by Abdo Publishing, a division of ABDO, PO Box 398166,
Minneapolis, Minnesota 55439. Copyright © 2018 by Abdo Consulting
Group, Inc. International copyrights reserved in all countries. No part of this
book may be reproduced in any form without written permission from the
publisher. Core Library™ is a trademark and logo of Abdo Publishing.

Printed in the United States of America, North Mankato, Minnesota
032017
092017

THIS BOOK CONTAINS
RECYCLED MATERIALS

Cover Photo: Bettmann/Getty Images
Interior Photos: Bettmann/Getty Images, 1, 19; dapd/AP Images, 4–5; Red Line Editorial, 7, 14;
AP Images, 9, 24; Library of Congress/Corbis Historical/VCG/Getty Images, 12–13; Fox Photos/
Hulton Archive/Getty Images, 17; US Navy/The LIFE Picture Collection/Getty Images, 22–23, 45;
Past Pix/SSPL/Getty Images, 26; Crown/Mirrorpix/Getty Images, 28–29; Bletchley Park Trust/SSPL/
Getty Images, 31; PhotoQuest/Archive Photos/Getty Images, 34–35; Universal History Archive/UIG/
Getty images, 38–39

Editor: Arnold Ringstad
Imprint Designer: Maggie Villaume
Series Design Direction: Nikki Farinella

Publisher's Cataloging-in-Publication Data

Names: Murray, Laura K., author.
Title: World War II technology / by Laura K. Murray.
Description: Minneapolis, MN : Abdo Publishing, 2018. | Series: War technology |
    Includes bibliographical references and index.
Identifiers: LCCN 2016962132 | ISBN 9781532111938 (lib. bdg.) |
    ISBN 9781680789782 (ebook)
Subjects: LCSH: United States--History--World War, 1939-1945--Technology--
    Juvenile literature. | Technology--United States--20th century--Juvenile
    literature.
Classification: DDC 940.53--dc23
LC record available at http://lccn.loc.gov/2016962132

CONTENTS

CHAPTER
ONE

LIGHTNING WAR

It was September 1, 1939. A shrieking siren filled the air. The German dive-bomber surged toward the ground. It aimed for the target below. Suddenly the pilot released the bomb. He pulled his plane's nose up and zoomed away. The bomb made an earsplitting whistling noise as it fell to Earth. Instantly, a Polish bridge exploded into flames. Debris shot in all directions. Giant plumes of smoke went into the air. More bombers appeared overhead. They were ready to rain destruction on Poland.

Elsewhere, German tanks barreled over the ground. They smashed through Polish lines.

German dive-bombers appeared in the skies over Poland as Germany launched its invasion.

Troops in trucks followed to trap the enemy. From a harbor, a German battleship fired its guns on a Polish city. Germany was using a tactic known as blitzkrieg, or lightning war. Blitzkrieg uses unexpected strikes to win a quick victory. It involves many advanced technologies. Powerful weapons overwhelm defenders. Radios allow the attackers to coordinate their invasion. Invading troops rush through enemy defenses. They paralyze their foes.

Poland's outdated equipment was no match for the blitzkrieg. The outnumbered Polish troops fought back fiercely. But in just over a month, Poland fell to Germany.

WAR BREAKS OUT

Soon after the invasion, the United Kingdom and France declared war on Germany. World War II (1939–1945) had begun. Many of the seeds for the conflict had been planted after World War I (1914–1918). Following that war, a losing Germany was punished harshly. In the

RESOURCES
OF POLAND AND GERMANY

Germany's military was much better equipped than Poland's in 1939. What do you notice about the numbers of tanks, aircraft, and soldiers each country deployed during the invasion? How does this help you understand Germany's quick takeover?

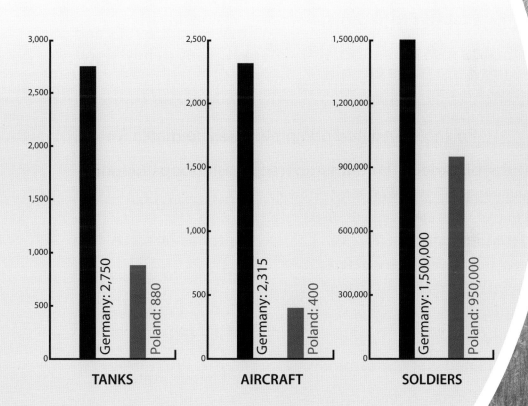

aftermath, Adolf Hitler rose to power. He promised to bring the German nation back to greatness. Hitler built up the nation's military. He triggered World War II when he ordered the invasion of Poland.

SECRET PREPARATION

The Treaty of Versailles ended World War I. It forced Germany to accept responsibility for the war. It limited the size of Germany's military. It also banned Germany from having submarines. However, Hitler ignored the treaty. He built up Germany's army. He created a new air force and navy. Before World War II, he began taking territory from other nations. No one stopped him.

World War II was fought by two groups. They were the Axis and the Allied powers. The Axis included Germany, Japan, and Italy. These nations were focused on expanding their territories by force. The major Allied powers included the United Kingdom, France, the United States,

Hitler oversaw a massive buildup of the German military in the 1930s.

GERMAN SCIENTISTS ON THE MOVE

Hitler and the Nazi Party were extremely racist and anti-Semitic. They called for the elimination of Jews and other minority groups. These beliefs hurt Germany's scientific progress. In the early 1930s, many Jewish scientists in Germany were fired. Hitler said, "If the dismissal of Jewish scientists means the end of contemporary German science, then we shall do without science for a few years." By 1944 more than 133,000 German Jews had fled to the United States. Many lent their talents to their new country's research.

the Soviet Union, and China.

World War II spanned the globe. Battles took place on land, in the air, and on the sea. Much of the action occurred in Europe and in the Pacific Ocean. World War II lasted until 1945. It became the deadliest war in history. More than 60 million soldiers and civilians died.

SCIENCE AND THE RACE TO VICTORY

World War II led to great advances in

technology. Researchers on both sides worked to win the war. One area of study was nuclear research. In 1945 the United States dropped two atomic bombs on Japan. Another key development was radar. It let the Allies detect distant enemy aircraft. These and other technologies of World War II changed the world forever.

EXPLORE ONLINE

Chapter One discusses the German tactic of blitzkrieg. Check out the website below for more information on this topic. How is the information from the website the same as the information in Chapter One? What new information did you learn from the website?

BLITZKRIEG (LIGHTNING WAR)

abdocorelibrary.com/world-war-ii-tech

TECHNOLOGY OVERHEAD

The Allied and Axis powers fought for control of the skies during World War II. Both sides raced to develop planes that could fly higher and faster. Airplane engineers worked to make new breakthroughs.

On the Axis side, dive-bombers gained a terrifying reputation. Germany's air force used the Ju 87 Stuka. Flying this plane, pilots could accurately strike small targets on the ground. The Stuka had a system that automatically pulled it out of its dive. This was important because the extreme forces could cause pilots to briefly black out.

During the war, vast US aircraft plants turned out huge numbers of bombers.

AIRCRAFT PRODUCTION

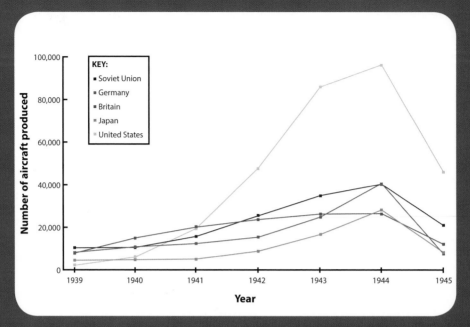

KEY:
- Soviet Union
- Germany
- Britain
- Japan
- United States

Number of aircraft produced / *Year*

The Allied and Axis powers raced to make the best aircraft during World War II. What do you notice about the number of aircraft produced by the main players? How does it help you understand the importance of air technology? What do you think is more important: quality or quantity?

From July to October of 1940, German and British fighter planes fought in the skies over the United Kingdom. This clash was the Battle of Britain. Germany tried to crush the Royal Air Force (RAF). This would clear the way for an invasion. But the RAF successfully fended off the Germans. The British Supermarine Spitfire outmatched the German Messerschmitt Bf109. Another

British fighter was the Hawker Hurricane. Pilots used it to shoot down hundreds of German aircraft.

ATTACK ON PEARL HARBOR

On December 7, 1941, 353 Japanese aircraft attacked the US naval base at Pearl Harbor, Hawaii. They included torpedo planes, dive-bombers, and fighters. The Aichi D3A Val and the Mitsubishi A6M Zero were among the Japanese planes. The aircraft had taken off from Japanese aircraft carriers near Hawaii.

Japan wanted to destroy the US Navy's Pacific fleet. This would allow Japan to expand its empire without American interference. The attacks sank or damaged all eight US battleships at Pearl Harbor. But the ships sank in shallow water. US troops were able to raise and repair some of them. Additionally, the US Navy's aircraft carriers were not at Pearl Harbor that day. These ships would let the US Navy strike back at Japan.

In response to the attack, the United States declared war on Japan. Germany, Japan's partner, then declared war on the United States. The United States had officially joined the Allies.

SUPER BOMBERS

In 1942 the Allies began using the Boeing B-17 Flying Fortress to bomb German cities. B-17s were four-engine bombers. They carried devices called Norden bombsights. Norden bombsights calculated where bombs would fall. They used the aircraft's speed and direction to produce accurate results. Extreme secrecy surrounded the advanced device. Bomber crews were ordered to destroy it if they landed in enemy territory. When a B-17 returned to base, the Norden bombsight was removed. Security forces stored it in a safe location.

In 1944 the Allies introduced the B-29 Superfortress. This giant bomber was a technological wonder. It was the first military aircraft with pressurized crew areas. Air was sealed inside the bomber. This protected the crew from extreme cold and thin air

The Pearl Harbor attack, made possible by Japanese aircraft carriers, thrust the United States into World War II.

FAILED INVENTIONS

Not all wartime ideas became a reality. For example, the Japanese attempted to develop a death ray. It worked a bit like a microwave oven. However, the design never moved past the testing stage. It was not the only unusual invention. The British worked on building ships out of ice. The United States hoped to use bats to carry small bombs. Hitler tried to make a compressed air cannon to shoot down Allied planes.

at high altitudes. Computers helped aim the bomber's defensive machine guns. B-29s flew bombing missions over Japan. They destroyed large parts of many Japanese cities.

JET ENGINES

Wartime engineers designed aircraft to go faster than ever before. Most of the war's aircraft had piston engines that spun propellers. By 1944 a new development was emerging: the jet engine. A jet engine takes in air and compresses it. Then it burns the air along with fuel. A stream of hot, high-speed gases flies out the back. This pushes the aircraft forward.

Me 262s shot down more than 500 Allied aircraft, but by the time the jets arrived they were too late to affect the war.

Germany's Messerschmitt Me 262 was the first jet fighter. It went into combat in 1944. The aircraft could reach speeds of 550 miles per hour (885 km/h). This was much faster than the Allies' fastest plane. However, the jet arrived too late to make an impact. Germany was unable to build many Me 262s. The technology needed more development. Jet engines were not widely produced until after the war.

ROCKET POWER

Germany grew desperate as it began losing the war. In 1944 it began to use its V-weapons, or vengeance weapons. These weapons launched bombs into Allied territory. They were unlikely to make a difference in the war. But they could strike with little warning. They were meant to terrify Allied civilians.

PERSPECTIVES
HUMAN COMPUTERS

During World War II, many US men were in the military. American women got involved in technology on the home front. They worked as human computers. Human computers were people who performed calculations. Their work helped soldiers accurately aim long-range artillery. After the war, human computers helped with the US space program.

The V-1 was a jet-powered flying bomb. The Allies were able to track V-1s using radar. Fighter planes and antiaircraft guns shot many of them down.

However, the V-2 was impossible to defend against. It was a long-range rocket.

It could fly more than 100 miles (161 km). The V-2 had an automatic guidance system. This system tracked the location of the V-2. It adjusted the rocket's course. The V-2 flew in a huge arc before falling on its target. It moved at several times the speed of sound. These rockets killed thousands of people.

V-2 attacks ended in 1945. Allied troops finally overran the launch sites. The V-2 was a deadly weapon during the war. However, its rocket technology had a peaceful use, too. It made future space travel possible.

FURTHER EVIDENCE

Chapter Two has information about World War II aircraft. What was one of the main points of this chapter? What key evidence supports this point? Read the article at the website below. Does the information on the website support the main point of this chapter? Does it present new evidence?

WORLD WAR II AIRPLANES

abdocorelibrary.com/world-war-ii-tech

BY LAND AND SEA

The Pacific Ocean lay between Japan and the United States. The English Channel lay between mainland Europe and the United Kingdom. To win the war, the Allies needed to control these waters. Then, their troops could land on enemy shores.

WATER BATTLES

In the Pacific, Japanese outposts dotted the vast ocean. The Allies used a strategy known as island-hopping. They captured some islands. These became new Allied bases. They also bypassed some islands entirely.

The overwhelming strength of the US Navy proved decisive in World War II.

A full load of aircraft gave carriers incredible firepower.

Some of the most important vessels were aircraft carriers. The *Essex*-class carriers made up the backbone of the US fleet. These huge ships were 874 feet (266 m) long. Each held 90 aircraft. The carriers also had antiaircraft guns to defend themselves. A total of 15 of these carriers went into battle. Some were hit by enemy fire, but none were sunk.

D-DAY LANDINGS

On June 6, 1944, Allied forces launched an invasion of Nazi-occupied Europe. Thousands of men landed on the beaches of Normandy, France. Warships and bombers pounded away at the coast.

More than 5,000 landing craft and ships were involved. Some of these craft were Higgins boats. They were made of wood and steel. When they reached shore, a ramp in front dropped down. The troops and equipment could quickly move onto the beach. The Allies took heavy casualties in the Normandy landings. But they were soon fighting their way across Europe.

ON THE GROUND

World War II troops had ground weapons of all kinds. One of the most important was the

PERSPECTIVES
EISENHOWER ON HIGGINS BOATS

US general Dwight Eisenhower believed the Higgins boats were critical to victory. In an interview after the war, he praised their designer: "Andrew Higgins is the man who won the war for us. . . . If Higgins had not designed and built [the boats], we never could have landed over an open beach. The whole strategy of the war would have been different."

Infantry and tanks advanced into battle together.

M1 Garand. US troops carried this rifle. Many rifles at the time had to be reloaded after each shot. This made firing slow and clumsy. But the M1 Garand could fire eight shots in a row. All a soldier had to do was keep pulling the trigger.

Most troops traveled on foot, but vehicles were also important. Tanks were some of the most powerful weapons on the battlefield. German tanks had thick armor and large guns. They often outmatched common Allied tanks, such as the Sherman.

However, advanced tanks didn't guarantee victory. Tanks had to be reliable. They also needed to be cheap enough to produce in large numbers. German tanks were expensive to build. They often broke down. A group of Shermans could surround and destroy a powerful German tank.

THE OSLO REPORT

In 1939 two mysterious letters arrived at the British Embassy in Oslo, Norway. They contained shocking information. The letters described secret German technology and weapons. They listed dive-bombers, electric fuses, flamethrowers, and more. They even gave the location of secret military labs. Most British officials believed the letters were fake. However, British intelligence officer Reg Jones believed they were real. He used the information as a guide throughout the war. The letters became known as the Oslo Report. Years later, the author was revealed to be German physicist Hans Ferdinand Mayer. Mayer wanted to see the Nazis defeated.

CHAPTER
FOUR

SUPPORT TECHNOLOGY

Weapons were not the war's only important technologies. A variety of support technologies also played key roles. They detected enemy planes, cracked codes, and kept soldiers healthy.

RADAR

Radar was one of the most important developments of World War II. Radar equipment sends out radio waves. These waves bounce off objects. The echoes travel back to the equipment. Operators use the echoes to determine the location of distant objects.

The closely guarded secrets of radar equipment were crucial to the Allied war effort.

THE RAD LAB

Most Allied radar was developed at the Radiation Laboratory, or Rad Lab. This laboratory was located at the Massachusetts Institute of Technology (MIT). The Rad Lab operated from 1940 until 1945. At its peak, the lab employed 3,500 people. Its scientists developed more than 100 radar systems.

Radar played a key role in the Battle of Britain. It gave advance warning of incoming aircraft. This helped the British plan an effective defense. Radar technology improved throughout the war. The Allies invested heavily in it.

CRACKING THE CODE

Codebreaking also played an important role. One example of this involved the German Enigma machines. These devices sent coded messages. The Germans believed their code could not be broken.

However, the Allies were able to crack the Enigma. The British called their secret codebreaking project "Ultra." As part of this effort, British scientists

The equipment used to break codes and analyze messages was highly complex.

developed the Bombe. This was a complex machine. It was based in part on an earlier Polish device. It searched for possible solutions to Enigma codes. By mid-1940, the Allies could read most German communications. By 1942 they had broken even Enigma's newest naval codes. This information helped the Allies avoid German submarines, called U-boats. These submarines attacked Allied vessels in the Atlantic. They hunted in groups. They were often able to sneak up on ships undetected. Breaking codes made it easier to defend against them.

MEDICINE

In earlier wars, infected wounds could quickly turn deadly. But starting in 1942, doctors used a substance

PERSPECTIVES
CODED LANGUAGE

Not all military codes relied on machines. Some Native Americans became known as code talkers. They developed secret codes in their native languages. Their work saved thousands of lives during World War II. Code talkers worked together to agree upon code words. This was because many military terms did not exist in their languages. Comanche code talker Roderick Red Elk recalled, "Somebody came up with an idea to call a tank a turtle. Somebody asked him why. He says, 'A turtle is like a tank. It's got a hard shell.'"

called penicillin to fight these infections. Penicillin was discovered in 1928. It is an antibiotic. It kills bacteria, keeping the patient healthy. The Allies produced massive amounts of penicillin.

The Pacific had unique health problems. Mosquitoes spread diseases such as malaria. US troops sprayed antimosquito chemicals into the air. The use of these chemicals helped slow the spread of disease.

STRAIGHT TO THE
SOURCE

In 1980 a US Navy officer wrote a report describing the impact of Ultra. In his conclusion, he said:

> It is without doubt valid to state that Ultra was to some degree an effective tool for the Allies in the Battle of the Atlantic. Whether or not the war was shorter because of it can only be speculated.
>
> Had it not been for the British and the fact that they were involved against the U-boat long before the United States entered the war, progress toward ultimate victory would have been far slower. Without a doubt the capture of the Enigma machine from U-110 by the British was the big break in Ultra in the early war years. The British efforts at Bletchley Park and at the Admiralty Tracking Room gave the United States a head start in organizing.

Source: Jerry Russell. "Ultra and the Campaign against U-Boats in World War II." *Naval History and Heritage Command*. US Navy, May 20, 1980. Web. Accessed January 16, 2017.

What's the Big Idea?
Read the passage carefully. What are the main ideas it presents? What guesses does it make about how the war could have gone differently?

THE ATOMIC BOMB

On May 7, 1945, the Germans surrendered. The Allies claimed victory in Europe. This became known as VE Day. However, the war in the Pacific continued. Japan was losing but refused to surrender. US president Harry S. Truman wanted to avoid a costly invasion. He ordered the use of a new technology: the atomic bomb.

THE MANHATTAN PROJECT

Six years earlier, in 1939, scientist Albert Einstein had written a letter to President Franklin Roosevelt. He said the Nazis were working on a powerful new bomb. The bomb

The atomic bomb would have a lasting impact to rival any other technology developed during World War II.

would split apart atoms. This would release huge amounts of energy.

Hearing this news, Roosevelt took action. He launched a joint effort with Britain to develop an atomic bomb first. This became known as the Manhattan Project. At its peak, it employed 130,000 people. The project was kept top secret. Even Truman, Roosevelt's vice president, did not learn of it until he became president in 1945.

The United States set up a laboratory in New Mexico. It was called Los Alamos. There, scientists developed two types of bombs. One used the element plutonium. The other used the element uranium.

On July 16, 1945, Manhattan Project scientists tested the first atomic bomb. The test was named Trinity. It took place in the New Mexico desert. The bomb, which used plutonium, was called the Gadget. A bright flash lit the night sky. A mushroom cloud rose high into the air. The bomb worked.

THE BOMBINGS OF HIROSHIMA AND NAGASAKI

On August 6, 1945, the American B-29 bomber *Enola Gay* took off from the island of Tinian. It flew over Hiroshima, Japan. The bomber dropped a uranium-type bomb on the city. It exploded with a giant flash of light and heat. The bomb killed approximately 135,000 people. Still, Japan did not surrender. On August 9, a B-29 called *Bockscar* dropped another atomic bomb. This one fell on the city of Nagasaki. It was a plutonium-type bomb.

PERSPECTIVES

EYEWITNESS TO THE A-BOMB

Physicist J. Robert Oppenheimer was the director of the Los Alamos lab. He watched the Trinity test alongside other scientists. They did not know what the bomb's power would mean for the future. Oppenheimer later said, "We knew the world would not be the same. A few people laughed. A few people cried. Most people were silent. I remembered the line from the Hindu scripture the *Bhagavad-Gita*. . . . 'Now I am become death, the destroyer of worlds.' I suppose we all thought that one way or another."

The Hiroshima bombing produced a towering mushroom cloud that rose thousands of feet into the air.

Approximately 50,000 people in the city died. Large portions of both cities were destroyed. On August 14, 1945, Japan announced its surrender. World War II had come to an end.

The full death toll of the bombs is difficult to estimate. After the initial blasts, many more people died from radiation poisoning. In some cases, the effects of radiation did not appear until years later.

A CHANGED WORLD

World War II launched an incredible scientific race. Around the globe, militaries used the talents of scientists and engineers. Many of their inventions still affect us today.

World War II resulted in a devastating number of civilian and military casualties. It also pushed humans to develop technology never before thought possible. Some new technologies brought more death. Others were invented to save lives. The war changed warfare and the world forever.

OPERATION PAPERCLIP

In May 1945, the United States began a secret program. It was known as Operation Paperclip. The program brought more than 1,600 German scientists, engineers, and technicians to the United States. They were not punished for helping the German war effort. Instead they were taken to do military research, including on rockets. Their work helped lay the groundwork for the US space program.

STRAIGHT TO THE
SOURCE

On August 6, 1945, president Harry S. Truman announced the atomic bombing of Japan. He credited Allied scientists for their work on the bomb:

The battle of the laboratories held fateful risks for us as well as the battles of the air, land, and sea, and we have now won the battle of the laboratories as we have won the other battles. . . . But the greatest marvel is not the size of the enterprise, its secrecy, nor its cost, but the achievement of scientific brains in putting together infinitely complex pieces of knowledge held by many men in different fields of science into a workable plan. And hardly less marvelous has been the capacity of industry to design, and of labor to operate, the machines and methods to do things never done before. . . . What has been done is the greatest achievement of organized science in history. It was done under pressure and without failure.

Source: "Press Release by the White House, August 6, 1945." *Truman Library & Museum*. Truman Library & Museum, n.d. Web. Accessed January 16, 2017.

Consider Your Audience

Adapt this passage as a blog post for a different audience, such as your principal or friends. How does your post differ from the original text and why? Do you agree with Truman?

IMPORTANT
DATES

1933
Adolf Hitler comes to power in Germany.

1930s
Nazi Germany dismisses thousands of Jewish scientists and others from their positions.

1939
Albert Einstein writes a letter to President Roosevelt warning him about German plans to build an atomic bomb.

1939
Germany invades Poland on September 1, marking the start of World War II.

1940
By October the United Kingdom's Royal Air Force defeats Germany's air force in the Battle of Britain.

1941
Japan attacks the US naval base at Pearl Harbor, Hawaii, on December 7.

1944

Germany begins using its V-1 and V-2 weapons against the Allies.

1944

Allied forces invade Europe during the D-Day landings on June 6.

1945

Germany surrenders on May 7, bringing an end to war in Europe.

1945

The US drops an atomic bomb on Hiroshima, Japan, on August 6. It drops a second atomic bomb on Nagasaki, Japan, on August 9.

1945

Japan announces its surrender on August 14, marking the end of World War II.

STOP AND
THINK

Tell the Tale
Chapter Three discusses the D-Day landings at Normandy. Imagine you are one of the troops arriving on the beaches in a Higgins boat. Write 200 words about the experience. Are you nervous? Confident? What does the war's technology mean to you as a soldier?

Surprise Me
Chapter Four discusses the supporting technology of World War II. After reading this book, what three facts about radar, codebreaking, or medicine did you find most surprising? Write a few sentences about each fact. Why did you find each fact surprising?

Dig Deeper
After reading this book, what questions do you still have about World War II aircraft or ships? With an adult's help, find a few reliable sources that can help you answer your questions. Then write a paragraph about what you learned.

You Are There

This book discusses codebreaking during World War II. Imagine you are a wartime codebreaker. Write a diary entry about your work. Why is this work important? How does technology affect your work? Would you prefer to fight on the frontlines or work in a support role?

GLOSSARY

anti-Semitic
prejudiced against
Jewish people

blitzkrieg
a type of German warfare
that uses technology and
rapid attacks to overwhelm
the enemy

casualties
troops that are killed,
wounded, or missing

civilians
people who are not in
the military

flamethrower
a weapon that shoots fire at
an enemy

penicillin
an antibiotic used to treat
bacterial infections

piston engines
engines that are powered
by cylinders moving up
and down

racist
having the belief that one
race is better than another

radiation
energy that is emitted as
waves or particles, produced
by nuclear reactions or
radioactive materials

LEARN MORE

Books

Conley, Kate. *World War II through the Eyes of Franklin Delano Roosevelt.* Minneapolis, MN: Abdo Publishing, 2016.

Hamilton, John. *World War II: Weapons.* Minneapolis, MN: Abdo Publishing, 2012.

Hawes, Alison. *Who's Who in WWII.* New York: Crabtree, 2011.

Websites

To learn more about War Technology, visit **abdobooklinks.com**. These links are routinely monitored and updated to provide the most current information available.

Visit **abdocorelibrary.com** for free additional tools for teachers and students.

INDEX

About the Author

Laura K. Murray has written more than 40 nonfiction books for children. She enjoyed learning all about World War II, in which her grandpa served. She lives in Minnesota.